CW00951644

Take My HAND

GIOVANNA GUTTA

Illustrated by STEFANIE ST.DENIS

Take My Hand

Tellwell Talent
www.tellwell.ca

ISBN
978-0-2288-3278-2 (Hardcover)
978-0-2288-3277-5 (Paperback)
978-0-2288-3279-9 (Ebook)

This story is dedicated to 4 of the greatest loves of my life! Without you, there's no me. You've all made me the woman I am today! Such a joy and a blessing to be your mom! I love you McKenzie Kennedy, Austino and Thai...

Love mommy (Roo Roo) ♥ XOXO

From the beginning
From the time you were born
To let you know I was happy and you were safe
I placed my fingers in the palm of your soft and tiny hand

Before you knew it

You were up and about Taking your first steps

One foot in front of the other With balance and poise

As you reached out and took my hand

A little bit older now Waking up from your sleep You yelled,

“Mommy, Mommy,

I had a bad dream!”

You’d come lay in my bed and Nuzzle up real close

And what brought you some comfort? You took my hand

SCHOOL

Before you knew it

It was your first day of school

You were excited but shy You said,

“Mommy I’m scared!”

So I kissed you on the forehead And
asked, “How can I help?”

You said, “Could you please hold my hand?”
And you gently took my hand

As time passed

You went through school and were so
involved in School events, sports, and

Instrumental too

I'd come pick you up and with so much to say
all about your day You'd take my hand

Oh my, how time flies

Oh, how you have grown

On to high school and then college,

A significant other and friends

And with each visit I knew you wouldn't be needing to take my hand as much Busy living life, working, travelling, family BBQs, and then the time had come,

For you to get married too!

You came to me and asked, “Mom? Would you
walk me down the aisle and give me away?”

I happily replied, “I won’t give you away,
but I’ll share you instead.”

You jumped with joy and hugged me real tight

Taking my hand as I said, “Lead the way!”

With joy in my heart and tears in my eyes,
I kissed you on your forehead

For the last time, you were completely all mine

I walked you down the aisle

Your hand in mine

As more time passed, you had kids of your own
And from the beginning, from the time she was
born, you Placed your fingers in the palm of
her soft, tiny hand and You took her hand

Before you knew it, she was taking her
first steps Happy and gleaming

One foot in front of the other to keep
her steady Balanced and poised

She reached for your hand And you took her hand

As you grew together with your family, you started to understand That taking her hand in all that she needs is an important bond And a very special love

As I have done with you, you have done the same

Passing on all the love I've shared with you through time, again and again

We've all grown together now: you, your family, and me.
A lifetime has gone by Mommy is much older now, you see

So it's hard to walk or stand or do much with ease

"It's okay, Mom," she says. "I got you! Don't worry,
you'll see! It's time I show you All the love you show me!"

So she puts out her arm and opens her hand and says,
"I would be honoured if you would take my hand."

THE END

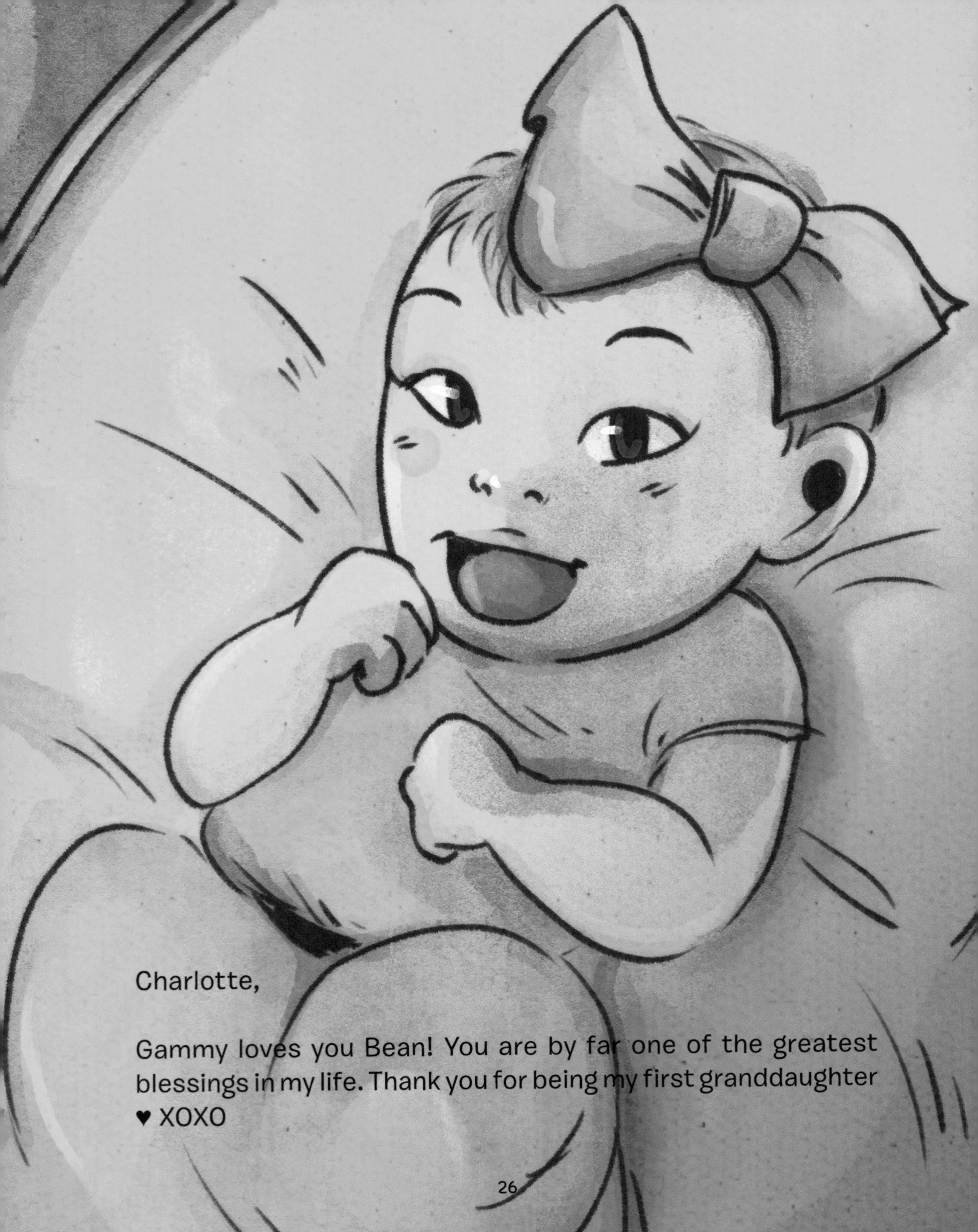

Charlotte,

Gammy loves you Bean! You are by far one of the greatest blessings in my life. Thank you for being my first granddaughter ♥ XOXO

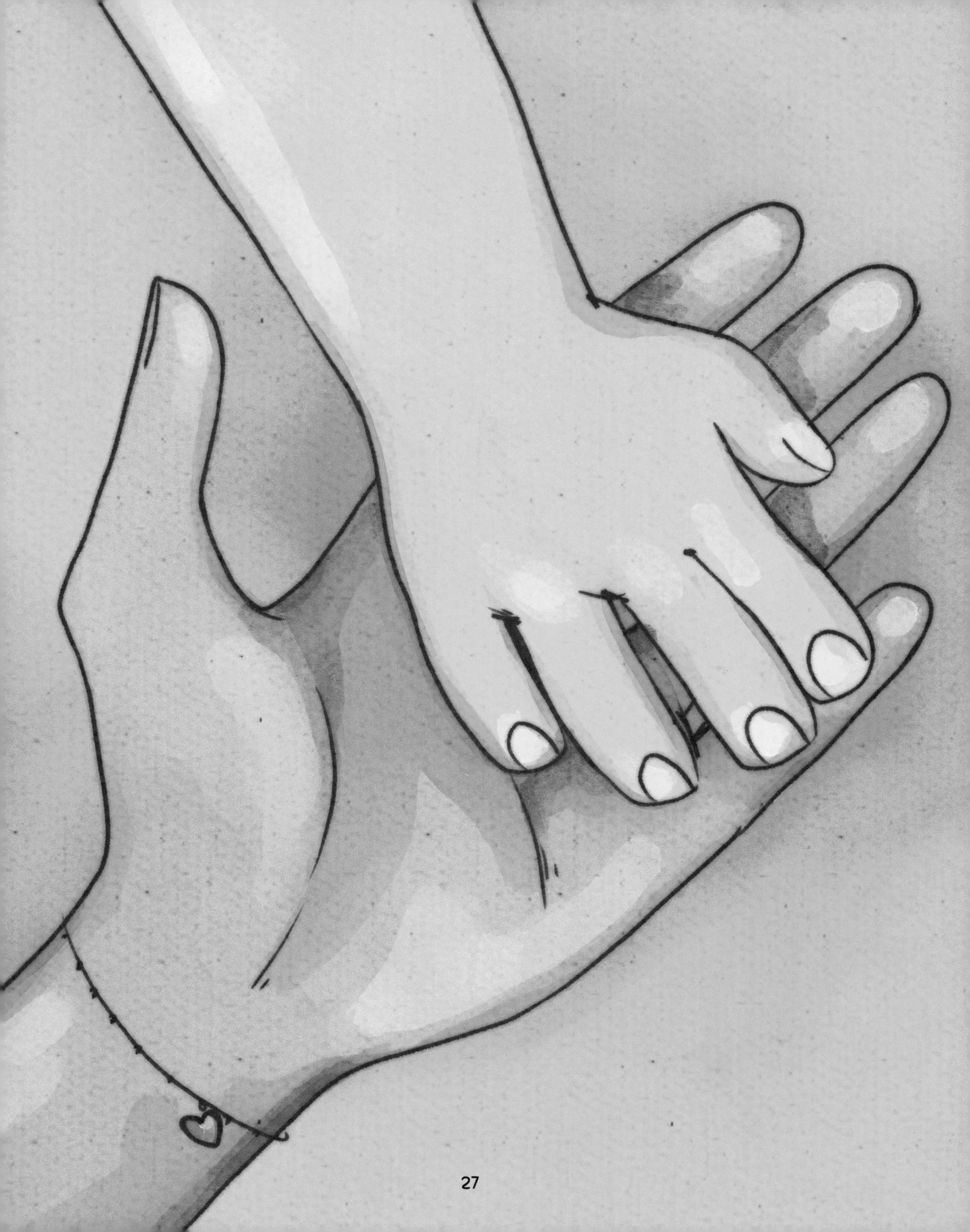